Operational
Anonymization

Operational Anonymization

REGAIN YOUR PRIVACY AND ANONYMITY

• • •

Scott R. Mayer

ISBN: 1548474029
ISBN-13: 9781548474027

I dedicate this book to my father, Barry A. Mayer, who worked his entire life at the same job to ensure that I would have no outstanding financial responsibilities. My father, through his actions, allowed me to take the risks that have led to my success today. I would like to thank my mother and father for all the opportunities they have provided me over the years and for guiding me down a path that led to my good health, wealth, and wisdom. Dad, I know you're watching; this one's for you.

Scott R. Mayer

Contents

Introduction

• • •

WHAT IS OPERATIONAL ANONYMIZATION?

OPERATIONAL ANONYMIZATION IS THE PROCESS of remaining private and secure while using the internet. It utilizes the same tricks and tools of the trade used by hackers and criminals to avoid detection and prosecution. Operational anonymization requires staying up to date with the latest tools and tactics. No one tool can define operational anonymization, as it is a cat-and-mouse game between hackers, governments, and private citizens. I will teach you through this book the current standards and tools used for operational anonymization. Although this book will help to keep you on the cutting edge for a substantial amount of time, it is up to you to stay current with the new tools and techniques as they are discovered and released. Operational anonymization currently includes the use of Tor, which is a tool used to conceal a user's identity; VPNs, which are tools used to protect sensitive data; PGP encryption, which is a method of encrypting messages and files; secure operating systems such as Qubes, which compartmentalizes your activities and secures them from any crossover in case of incursion into one of these activities qubes; and live operating systems such as Tails and Whonix, which help anonymize and protect users and their data. These tools, along with the tricks and tactics I'll teach you, should be sufficient for keeping you anonymous and private from even the most sophisticated of spies, including hackers, competitive companies, and even governments.

Operational anonymization is for everybody, whether you're a whistleblower, a public or private company, or a private citizen. This book includes everything you need to know in order to stay private and safe. The US government's defensive stance during its global mass-surveillance program was that citizens were trading their privacy for security. I believe that this should have been each individual's choice. Yes, some people will likely use the information in this book to do bad things, but they would have found ways to do those things anyway—where there's a will, there's a way. This book is for the honest people who may not have had the knowledge or the connections to obtain the same information that people who do illegal things use every day to stay private and secure. Why should one group of people be privy to the information that could keep us all anonymous and safe and not everyone else?

Revealed to the public every single day are new hacks, data breaches, invasions of privacy, and nude celebrity photos, all of which are the result of mass hacks and data leaks. If you open a newspaper on any given day, you'll read about ransomware attacks on schools, hospitals, businesses, and private citizens. This particular collection of malicious code attacks a user's documents, pictures, music, videos, and so on, and then holds them ransom for money. If, for some reason, the victims are unable to pay—whether it be because they don't have the money or because they're unfamiliar with how to buy Bitcoin—then their data will be deleted for good. Many people have lost photos from the past of their loved ones or job résumés they've worked on and kept up to date for years. Everyone believes that this will not happen to them until it does, and then they take action only after the fact. Sometimes it's simply too late to do anything about it. Do not wait until this has happened to you. Do not be a victim. Do everything you can to protect yourself, your data, and your family right now.

This book will teach you the methods of operational anonymization, which will allow you to browse the web, communicate, make purchases, do business, and live a digital life devoid of being watched during your every action and communication. I have become an expert on operational anonymization by submerging myself in the dark net and belonging to and using hacker forums, dark net markets, and other anonymous resources to gain a complete understanding of the tools, tips, and tricks that criminals and hackers use for impure purposes. I have dissected, analyzed, and simplified these methods and have made them accessible and implementable by all private citizens and businesses interested in using them to live more private lives. These tricks, tips, techniques, and tools have kept well-known hackers and groups, such as the many members of Anonymous, out of the hands of even the most technologically savvy of entities, including the FBI, the NSA, and the CIA. Later in this book, you'll learn to use some of the same tools wielded by secret groups, freedom fighters, and individuals. Members of these groups are grossly intelligent and constantly revising and modifying their security. I'm not here to discuss whether or not you believe these groups are good or bad, or if you believe in what they do. I'm here so that you, too, can lead an anonymous life on the internet, whether you're an activist, a whistleblower, or just a citizen who both likes the idea of anonymity and deserves the privacy and security the US Constitution (and other governing documents for those who live elsewhere) has promised you. You, too, can master operational anonymization.

HOW SHOULD I USE THIS BOOK?

This book will break down the tools and techniques that individuals and businesses can use to stay anonymous on the internet and keep themselves safe and secure from hackers, breaches, and from being spied on by individuals, companies, and governments. Each chapter breaks down a specific group of tools, tips, and techniques. You don't need to read this book from cover to cover to benefit from it. Read what chapters relate to you and learn about the tools and tricks you've never heard of or that will benefit you or your company to the greatest extent. If you find that a chapter, technique, or tool is unnecessary or doesn't suit your business or personal needs, then skip it. There's no need for you to be bored. Why read something that doesn't apply to you?

WHO ISN'T THIS BOOK FOR?

If you're one of those people who believe that you have nothing to hide, then this book is not for you. I'm not here to debate whether or not your privacy is worth less than your security. No one has debunked this statement better than Glenn Greenwald of the *Guardian*, who has spoken on the topic numerous times over the years since the Edward Snowden NSA leak. Whenever he encounters people who use the "I have nothing to hide" defense, he pulls out a pen and paper and asks them to give him all their personal email addresses and passwords. He makes sure to stress that he doesn't just want the respectable work email addresses; he wants them all so that he can search through whatever it is they're doing online, whatever they're reading, and whatever they're looking at in order to publish anything he finds of interest online for the world to see. Not a single person to date has taken him up on this offer. We all have something to hide.

DISCLAIMER

Whether or not you agree with the NSA's massive surveillance program, we can all agree that it is the largest and most documented example of a hack that most people will understand. It is because of this widespread knowledge of that hack that I will use examples from the NSA's mass-surveillance program to express ideas and tools in a way that the vast majority of people will understand. The information you're about to read is based on documented facts. It will be up to you to decide whether you believe Snowden's leak was right or wrong and whether or not you believe it was (and still may be) necessary. I have not written this book to modify your beliefs; this book is simply a tool to inform individuals and businesses about how they can protect themselves from hackers, thieves, and other criminals who employ these techniques every single day to get people's most private and important information.

THANK YOU

The 2nd amendment of the Constitution of the United States of America is there to provide us the ability to overthrow an oppressive government should the need arise. The second amendment to the Constitution states "A well regulated Militia, being necessary to the security of a free State, the right of the people to keep and bear Arms, shall not be infringed."

The Declaration of Independence strengthens this fact by declaring "when a long train of abuses and usurpations, pursuing invariably the same Object evinces a design to reduce them under absolute Despotism, it is their right, it is their duty, to throw off such Government."

When our "founding fathers" were having meetings to plan the Independence of the United States of America they met in private. The necessity of privacy was because if the "founding fathers" were discovered to be having secret meetings to overthrow the government, they would have been captured and most likely killed. If the British government had the technology back then, that the United States has today, the revolution would have never occurred, and we would still be under British rule. If you love this country and all that America stands for, then you can thank privacy and anonymity for allowing or "founding fathers" to write history

If it is our right, our duty to rise against an oppressive government, then it is essential to be able to communicate privately and anonymously. Privacy needs to be a fundamental right under the most basic of laws of our country based on both the Constitution and the Declaration of Independence.

Our government is full of generally decent people, but just like with any profession there are a few bad apples. There are enough corrupt officials, with enough power, that most employees that are working government jobs will just sit down, shut up, and obey orders out of fear. Their concern includes fear of being dragged through the mud in the media, fear of being unjustly harassed and embarrassed in front of constituents, and fear of being arrested and imprisoned like those who publicly spoke out before them.

Thank you for reading this guide focused on reclaiming your privacy and anonymity online. I have put much time and effort in putting together this guide for all of you, but I couldn't have done it without inspiration from many security forums in which most people are anonymous. Many things I have learned and have, in turn, taught come from the hard working men and woman behind Privacytools.io which are crowd sourced information through a Reddit forum. An anonymous person who is known only as Jolly

Rodger who has been offline and unable to be reached for a proper thank you has inspired me with his take on security and privacy.

"Privacy Tools | Encryption against Global Mass Surveillance." Privacytools.io. Accessed July 08, 2017. https://privacytoolsio. github.io/privacytools.io/.

Rodger, Jolly. "Jolly Roger's Security Thread for Beginners." The Hub. January 15, 2014. Accessed July 08, 2017. http://thehub7xbw4dc5r2.onion/index.php?topic=52.0.

CHAPTER 1

Mass Surveillance and the Fourteen Eyes

• • •

MANY OF YOU MAY NOT know who or what the five eyes are, let alone who and what the fourteen eyes are. So let's start with the five eyes, which include the United Kingdom, the United States, Australia, Canada, and New Zealand. These five countries came to a collaborative agreement to collect, analyze, and share information on one another's citizens, corporations, and public data. Each of these members focuses on data analysis and collection in different parts of the world. In this agreement, each country has also promised not to spy on one another and not to act as adversaries regarding digital surveillance. The agreement does not mean, however, that these countries do not spy on one another's citizens—just not on one another's governments. The agreement is a means to avoid breaking laws that prohibit spying on their citizens. US security officials refer to this group as the United States' inner circle of closest allies who don't need to spy on one another.

The five eyes also have agreements with other countries to spy on their citizens, but these agreements do not specify that they would not spy on one another; they often have and continue to do so. These nine additional countries include Denmark, France, the Netherlands, Norway, Belgium, Germany, Italy, Spain, and Sweden.

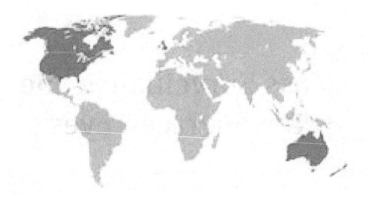

Because of the US-based surveillance program, it is generally not recommended for private citizens or companies in search of privacy and operational anonymity to use services based in the United States. Not using US-based services is in part due to the use of national security letters, also known as NSLs. The US uses NSLs when the surveillance program and its operators decide a company or service needs to build a back door; these companies are served an NSL and accompanying gag order, which prohibits the company from disclosing information about the request.

One of the largest examples of the use of NSLs and gag orders is the case of Lavabit, which was a secure email service that intentionally kept absolutely no logs of interactions between individuals and no logs of the interactions themselves. This practice made it impossible for Lavabit to comply with any orders to hand over information. When the FBI discovered that Snowden had been using this company to send emails, they requested a record of all his activities. Because Lavabit does not track or keep this information, the company was unable to comply with the FBI's request. Viewing this inability to provide the requested information as an act of defiance, the FBI served a subpoena with a gag order demanding an SSL key (essentially a digital lock that allows a secure connection to a website) be handed over that would grant the FBI backdoor access to communication and metadata in real time. Such access would provide real-time information about files and messages—such as who sent them, who created them, the GPS coordinates of where pictures were taken, the types of devices used to create them, and much more—of all of Lavabit's customers, including Snowden. Lavabit fought this demand in court in an attempt to get the case unsealed and to warn its customers that the privacy they had been promised and ensured through this service would soon be compromised. When Lavabit lost its last appeal, the company decided it was better to shut down than to compromise and expose its users. Lavabit's owner, Ladar Levison, was threatened with arrest when the US government determined that shutting down the service was a violation of its court order.

The FBI has not been here

(watch very closely for the removal of this sign)

Once businesses and the public became aware of these NSLs and gag orders, website owners and businesses developed a way to inform the public if they had been compromised. These became known as warrant canaries. A warrant canary is an image posted on a website stating that the FBI has not yet been there. If the FBI or any other agency force the company to comply with an order, the warrant canary is then removed from the page, thus allowing people to know that the company has been forced to comply with an order from the government that would compromise the security and privacy of its users. It later became illegal to remove a warrant canary from a site to warn the public of the site's compromised state, so websites gave warrant canaries expiration dates and renewed them regularly; their failure to be renewed was equivalent to them not being there at all.

CHAPTER 2

Tor and Virtual Private Networks

• • •

THE US GOVERNMENT HAS CONTRACTS with every major company and internet service provider (ISP). The government surveillance programs that whistleblowers such as Edward Snowden and Bill Binney have brought to light have the ability to track, monitor, record, and store data for later use. Collected data is not only your metadata but every message, picture, video, document, email, text message, and phone call you have ever sent, received, or viewed on the internet. You need to protect your data before it reaches these companies. One way to do this is to use a combination of Tor (the software program "The Onion Router") and a virtual private network, or VPN.

Tor is a tool that aims to conceal a user's identity and to privatize that specific user's online activity from surveillance and traffic analysis. It does this by separating identification as well as the route by which your information travels the internet. Your communications are encrypted and randomly bounced through a network of relays run by volunteers around the globe. When your data is first transmitted, it is encrypted with multiple layers; as it passes from relay to relay, the layers are peeled off like an onion, giving "The Onion Router" its name.

Whether or not you're using Tor, you should be using a VPN 100 percent of the time, especially when you're using the internet out in public. Think about every time you've connected to a public network and received the warning that any requests sent over this network are vulnerable. In addition to the fact that anybody who's using public Wi-Fi can monitor your activities on the network, ISPs are now capable of tracking and selling your data. A good VPN can hide your internet activity from your provider. It can also hide the fact that you are using Tor, which some companies and government agencies attempting to look at your data consider a red flag. Having said that, not all VPNs are created equal, and you should do your homework so that you'll get a good VPN that will keep you secure.

When choosing a VPN, you want to choose one that uses at least 128-bit encryption. 128-bit encryption will stop the majority of eavesdroppers, but you can get even higher levels of encryption, such as a 256-bit encryption. Another thing to be aware of is that some VPNs do keep logs. VPNs can turn these logs over to officials if they are asked to (or if they're hacked into), which can compromise your security. It is important to find a VPN that does not keep any logs of your activity. It doesn't matter what you're doing on the internet or whether it is right or wrong; no company will go to jail for the sake of a twenty-dollars-a-month subscriber, so if a VPN is keeping your logs, it will hand them over if asked.

One thing that's important to note is that, if you're using a VPN as a whistleblower or as a data leaker, it is vital to be conscious of what you type in over your VPN. Some VPNs claim not to keep logs of your data but in fact do. In cases like this, if you have typed your address into Google over that VPN or logged into your personal Facebook account, that address will be in the logs.

So let's talk about using Tor in combination with a VPN. By using a VPN, you're hiding your internet usage from your internet service provider. By doing this alone, your VPN still knows who you are. By combining Tor and a VPN, you're hiding your internet usage from your internet service provider while also hiding your final destination from the VPN. If you use Tor, then the VPN does not know your real IP address. Even if the VPN keeps logs of your activities, it can only identify you as an anonymous Tor user so long as you did not purchase your VPN service with a credit card or PayPal account. I will discuss how to make anonymous transactions in a later chapter.

Another advantage of combining Tor and a VPN is that, if your VPN connection drops, you'll still be connecting to the internet through Tor, and your real IP address will not be visible. On the other hand, government agencies sometimes set up compromised Tor nodes; doing so allows them to decrypt your traffic. If you're using a VPN as well, your traffic will remain safe. Remember:

Tor—anonymity—protects you.

VPN—privacy—protects your data.

I cannot stress enough how important it is to be aware of what you're typing, even if you are using Tor and a VPN. Extreme caution is necessary for certain situations, such as if you're leaking data, whistleblowing, or living in a censored country. Do not check your personal  Facebook or email accounts when using a VPN if this describes you. Facebook and Google log everything you do and voluntarily give this information to the US government. Instead of using Google, Bing, or Yahoo!—all of which give away your information to companies for advertising revenue and to government agencies for spying purposes—use a search engine that does not store personal information about you, such as DuckDuckGo (http://www.duckduckgo.com/) or StartPage (http://www.startpage.com/).

CHAPTER 3

What Web Browser Do You Use?

• • •

THE WEB BROWSER THAT YOU use can play a big role in your privacy and security. Have you ever noticed that ads seem to follow you from page to page, and you end up seeing something you were viewing last week over and over in your everyday computer usage? This ad placement is because every web browser tracks and monitors your traffic and data. You can use a variety of configurations and tools to make your web browser safer and more private, but two, in particular, stand out.

 The first web browser that stands out is Mozilla Firefox. Firefox is fast, reliable, and open-source, and the company respects your privacy. Although Firefox is all of these things, it is still not perfect. Many modifications and configurations are generally recommended when a user intends to be private and invisible. Some of the things that make Firefox dangerous are not even a part of Firefox. For example, JavaScript, which is necessary on many current websites, has been a popular target for hackers, who have discovered many vulnerabilities. You should completely disable JavaScript when using your web browser.

You can disable JavaScript by installing an add-on in your web browser called No Script Security Suite. Once No Script Security Suite is installed, you'll want to select the option to block scripts globally. Some pages, such as Netflix, require Java to run. No Script Security Suite has options to allow scripts on specific sites; just remember, though, that any site can be targeted through JavaScript vulnerabilities to exploit your computer and wreak havoc.

The latest vulnerability in JavaScript leaks your IP address, even if you're using a VPN. The vulnerability is known as WebRTC IP leaking. WebRTC is a communication protocol that uses JavaScript and can reveal your true IP address. I have included below slightly edited instructions from the internet on how to disable this protocol.[1]

How to disable WebRTC in Firefox? In short, you want to set "media.peerconnection.enabled" to "false" in "about:config."

Here's how:

Enter "about:config" in the Firefox address bar and press Enter.
Press the button "I'll be careful, I promise!"
Search for "media.peerconnection.enabled."
Double-click the entry; the column "Value" should now be "false."
You're now done. Do the WebRTC leak test again.

If you want to make sure every single WebRTC-related setting is really disabled, change these settings:

---

1 Mozilla. "Build Technology Idea Submission [Hide IP]." Issue #2. Mozilla/ TBTWBuildChallenge. GitHub. Accessed July 8, 2017. https://github.com/ mozilla/TBTWBuildChallenge/issues/2.

media.peerconnection.turn.disable = true
media.peerconnection.use_document_iceservers = false
media.peerconnection.video.enabled = false
media.peerconnection.identity.timeout = 1

Now you can be 100 percent sure WebRTC is disabled.

Several add-ons are also available that make Firefox more secure and excellent regarding privacy. These add-ons include the following:

uBlock Origin. This is an ad blocker that only minimally and almost undetectably affects the performance and speed of the web browser. It is completely open-source and free. Although I highly recommend the use of Firefox, uBlock also works with other browsers such as Safari, Opera, and Chrome.

Self-Destructing Cookies. This add-on automatically deletes cookies once you close a tab and the cookies are no longer needed. Cookies are used to track and monitor your usage to present you with ads; they may be used to spy on you, provide information on your traffic patterns, and share information (such as what site you have left to enter another site).

HTTPS Everywhere. This add-on automatically elevates your browsing to an HTTPS site when it is available. Many websites offer an HTTPS version; some sites offer this option exclusively. HTTPS encrypts your traffic to make it harder for someone who intercepts your traffic to decrypt it. One such example of use would be on websites where you enter your banking information online.

Once you have done all of these things to your Firefox browser, you can consider your browser safe for regular use.

The second web browser that stands out isn't another web browser but a previously modified version of Firefox. The Tor browser is your best choice when you need an extra layer of anonymity. The Tor browser comes preinstalled with all the privacy add-ons, encryption, and advanced proxy settings—settings used to access other computers to be used as hubs to get to your final destination—required to keep you safe and anonymous when using the internet. The Tor browser is easy to download and install. Once installed, the Tor browser requires no setup and is as simple as opening a regular web browser. The Tor browser also keeps you safe by automatically looking for an update each time you open it. This guarantees that anytime a vulnerability is discovered, you will have the latest update almost immediately. I believe it goes without saying, but the Tor browser utilizes "The Onion Router" network to anonymize your traffic and keep you safe from spying eyes.

While I'm on the subject of web browsers, I should talk about an important subject known as browser fingerprinting. Browser fingerprinting is the process by which you can be identified by features of your web browser that are recorded by websites. This includes information such as the browser you're using, the version of the browser, what add-ons you have installed, the size of your window (never use full screen, because that gives away information about your physical machine), the fonts you have installed, and the version number of all of your installed tools and extensions. Enough information is here to identify you as the same user at multiple websites. You can use a tool called Panopticlick to test if your browser is giving away your identity, and you can use several add-ons to help manipulate your browser's fingerprint. To name a few, you should be using Privacy Badger, an add-on that blocks advertisers and other third-party programs from tracking and monitoring you; uBlock Origin, an add-on for blocking pop-ups; and Disconnect, an add-on that blocks websites from monitoring your search and browsing history.

CHAPTER 4

Encrypted Email

• • •

ONE OF THE MAIN PARTS of the NSA's mass surveillance system was the collection of bulk emails, both international and domestic. The NSA had a back door into every major email carrier and was able to intercept and read every email of billions of US and non-US citizens. The NSA was able to choose specific keywords to filter for and could check to see if these keywords have been used in previous emails in its database; the agency could even set up notifications of when specific keywords are used in the future. The NSA could do the same thing with information specific to an individual user, such as a unique password that only you use or by a specific grammatical phrase that you use frequently. This information can then be used to link your identity to websites that you may have used different usernames on. This program looks for common spelling mistakes specific to certain individuals as well as specific patterns of speech and language.

One of the best ways to protect your email is a form of encryption known as PGP, which stands for "pretty good privacy" and is the current standard for encrypting files and messages. Once a message is encrypted, you can send it through any email or messaging server you want.

Here's how it works. First, you create a private key and a public key. The public key is the key you give out to people you want to send you encrypted messages; you keep your private key. This private key is the only key that can unlock messages that you've previously locked with your public key.

An example used by many is to think about a public key as one that can go around locking boxes that are intended for only you. Anyone can *lock* a box that is intended for you, but you are the only one with the key to unlocking the box. Even the person who sent you a message (i.e., locked a box) with your public key cannot unlock it. Only the person who possesses the private key can unlock it. If you wish to respond to this person, then you must use the person's public key to encrypt the message you intend to send. And that person uses his or her private key to decrypt the message.

Even if the messages were to get intercepted, or the servers that the messages went through were to be seized or hacked, the messages would be unreadable, as they are encrypted and decrypted at the user's level.

When creating a key, keep in mind that others may see the information associated with that key. Never use a private email address or a real name when creating a privacy key. Believe it or not, this has been the cause of more than one breach of data. Why give hackers or other snooping eyes any free insight into what you're doing?

This process does not have to be a long, complicated one. Many programs are available to automatically encrypt and decrypt messages, which makes the process simple and easy for almost anyone to implement. Overlooking such an easy thing to do that could save you millions of dollars as well as time spent on research and development is more than merely an oversight these days. I think it contributes to the hackers themselves.

Encrypting communications sounds like a complicated process, but in fact, it is pretty easy; there are many programs out there that make it even easier. Some programs go so far as to encrypt messages and decrypt messages for you and automatically share public keys with people you add to your friends list. One of the best examples of these programs is known as Pidgin with the add-on OTR, which stands for "off the record."

Just as with VPNs, email providers are not all created equal. The following is a list of email providers that offer more security and are more privacy conscious than others.

FREE

Name	Bitcoin	Encryption	Own Domain?
ProtonMail.com	Accepted	Built-In	Yes
Tutanola.com	No	Built-In	Yes
Mailfence.com	Accepted	Built-In	Yes

PAID

Name	Bitcoin	Encryption	Own Domain?
Mailbox.org	Accepted	Built-In	Yes
Posteo.de	No	Built-In	No
Runbox.com	No	No	Yes
Neomailbox.com	Accepted	Built-In	Yes
CounterMail.com	Accepted	Built-In	Yes
StartMail.com	No	Built-In	Yes
KolabNow.com	Accepted	No	Yes
CryptoHeaven.com	No	Built-In	Yes

Q ProtonMail   I use Proton Mail's premium version for a few dollars a month for both my personal and business email needs.

Most of these email providers have PGP built in, but if you choose one that does not (or you would like to use your current email address and provider), then you can still manually encrypt your messages. One of the easiest and most portable tools you can use is gpg4usb, which is a small and portable application that you can use to encrypt and decrypt any message or file on any Windows or Linux operating system.

If you use a desktop email client (which downloads your emails to your computer so you can access them locally) instead of a web-based email client (which you would need to ac-cess through the internet), then you can get an add-on such as Enigmail, which works with both Thunderbird (by the same developers as Firefox) and Seamonkey. Using Enigmail will allow you to write and receive encrypted messages effortlessly with PGP standards. Using a desktop email client is a really good idea, as leaving emails in the cloud makes it easier for hackers, spies, and governments to access them. Enacted laws in the United States now make emails older than six months considered abandoned and obtainable without a warrant. My two recommendations for a desktop mail manager are Mozilla Thunderbird and Claws Mail. Both are open-source and open to public scrutiny. Thunderbird also functions as a news feed, a newsgroup, and a chat client that supports XMPP, IRC, and Twitter. Claws Mail makes it extremely simple for new users, as it incorporates gpg4win and an encryption suite for Windows. It's packed with an abundance of features that everyone will find useful, such as email templates, built-in image viewer, drag 'n' drop support, dynamic signatures, anti-phishing URL checker, on-the-fly encryption and signing, and more.

If you're using a desktop application to encrypt and decrypt messages and files, *do not* store your private key on the computer. If someone steals or seizes your computer, that person will have your private key, and you will not, so he or she will be able to unlock all past and future messages. Even if you do gain access to your email accounts from elsewhere, you won't be able to decode your messages. Keep multiple copies of your keys in different locations in case of flood or fire or other damage to the storage medium, such as a USB flash drive or SD memory card.

CHAPTER 5

Secure Your Smartphone

• • •

THE NSA'S MASS-SURVEILLANCE PROJECT STARTED out just monitoring phone calls, but it expanded greatly from there to cover text messages and emails and then every piece of digital information that was sent or received in almost every part of the world. Just like emails, your text messages and phone calls are subject to the same keyword and key-phrase searches. Everything is transcribed and saved in text and full digital-media versions. That is, of course, unless you are using an encrypted messaging application. Encrypted messaging programs do not fully protect you, as both Google and Apple, the two largest companies in mobile operating systems, have built in back doors for government agencies that criminals have learned to exploit. For this reason, the first thing you'll learn about in this chapter is open-source mobile operating systems.

Everyone has heard about jailbreaking iPhones and rooting Androids, a procedure that allows you to install unofficial software on the device; these things have been around for a very long time. Numerous open-source operating systems are out there for each phone, many of which are focused on security and privacy. When people ask me if this is necessary, I always explain to them how information is the biggest moneymaker for Google, which is the largest mobile platform across numerous types of devices, including smartphones. Google spends billions of dollars every single year building up its data centers. The company also designs and builds many apps for the public, all of which are virtually free. Despite the amount Google spends each year on data centers and app development, the company turns tens of billions of dollars' worth of profit every year. How? Google sells your data and information to the highest bidder. Your information is so invaluable that it allows the company to give away almost everything for free.

 Let's use my personal favorite mobile operating system as an example, as I can speak from experience with using it. If you do a search for "secure Android OS," you'll find many that will work for whichever phone version you have. These secure mobile OSs have built-in encryption and security features, but most lack one thing: you won't have access to Google's Play Store and all the apps that are constantly monitoring and sending your data back to Google, but many open-source and private apps will replace almost any app you're used to using. It's very hard to adjust to one of these operating systems once you've become so accustomed to (and reliant on) all of Google's apps and tools, but if you're serious about your security and privacy, then you'll understand why it is important to cut these apps out of your daily use. The less information you freely give up, the more security and privacy you'll be able to protect from prying eyes.

If you're not ready to make the full jump to a secure operating system, you can use tools to help encrypt your messages, phone calls, and even video calls. Despite how well these tools encrypt your communications, your communications will still be subject to interception if you're under investigation or a government or hackers exploit your phone at a point before the message is encrypted. For example, keyloggers may be installed that intercept everything users type into their phones before an app has the opportunity to encrypt the message or password. That being said, let's examine some of these tools.

Signal. Developed by Open Whisper Systems, this instant-messenger app provides encrypted messaging and phone conversations. All communications are encrypted end-to-end. Signal is free and open-source, which allows security experts globally to constant access to audit the program to determine how secure the code is. Signal is completely free and does not monetize its app with ads. The company has gained such a reputation for encrypted messages that the US Senate has approved its use for all staff as of May 2017.

Wire. Developed by Wire Swiss GmbH, this app allows users to exchange encrypted instant messages, phone calls, and video calls. Wire is another free open-source app that allows for mass-security auditing by professionals. Unlike Signal, Wire monetizes its services with in-app purchases of premium features and services. Wire is also available as a computer application on the Windows and Mac operating systems.

Ricochet. This app uses the Tor network to hide your location and IP address. It is a computer application that is available on Windows, Linux, and Mac OSX. Ricochet avoids messaging servers and avoids logging of conversations. Instead of a username, you are given an address along the lines of *"ricochet:rs7ce36jsj24ogfw."* Other users must use this address to add you as a contact to their lists, and vice versa.

Linphone. This is an open-source phone app more commonly referred to as VOIP (or voice-over internet protocol) that is used to transmit audio in the form of a phone call over the internet instead of through a phone carrier, thus allowing for end-to-end encrypted phone calls and video communications.

As I mentioned before, none of these are full-encryption solutions, but each of these tools will go a long way in keeping your information safe from lurking eyes and government spies.

CHAPTER 6

Encrypted File Storage and File Shredding

• • •

I HAVE ADDRESSED HOW TO get your files from one point to another without them being unlocked or read by anyone, but how do you keep them safe when they are exactly where you want them to be? For that, I rely on hard-drive and file encryption.

It doesn't matter what operating system you are running; if I were to pull your hard drive from your computer and plug it into another machine, I would be able to browse your files freely and with full administrative permission. Doing so bypasses the need for even a simple login and password. Relying on only a windows password is the most insecure way to save files, and yet it seems that this is what everyone does. Everyone assumes that if you put a lock on it, then it must be secure. The only true way to protect your data is to encrypt it.

"Full disk encryption" will protect your drive from the people who may gain access one day. It does this by formatting your drive and rewriting the file system in an encrypted fashion so that it can only be accessed with the decryption key. If you lose your decryption key, there is no recovery. Your only choice is to format the drive and start over again. So make sure you remember it!

Where do you store your decryption key? This decryption key is the digital equivalent of handing over the keys to a castle. If someone were to get your encryption key, that person could begin to dissect every file you have and every message you have ever received. I recommend you store your PGP keys, decryption keys, and other sensitive data on an SD card or USB so that if that day comes when you're compromised and you get a knock at your door, you'll have time to dispose of that SD card or USB quickly. Always prepare for the day when "they" might come for you.

For local full disk encryption, VeraCrypt is the only open-source program (both paid and free) that is compatible with all the latest operating systems, including at the time of writing Windows 10 Redstone 2 Version 1703. VeraCrypt can encrypt anything from a portable flash drive to your entire operating system and all its components.

I understand that storing files locally on your hard drive may not be the best option for everyone. For those who prefer to keep files accessible from anywhere, encrypted clouds allow you to store files online to be forever accessible from anywhere, at any time, on any device. Just remember that, if for any reason the company hosting your data is taken down or goes out of business, your data will be lost and unrecoverable. Two great examples of these services are Seafile and Least Authority S4.

 *Seafile.* This open-source program allows you to store information in the cloud or to host your own server. With Seafile, your data is stored on a server in Germany (or with Amazon web services in the United States for the cloud version).

Seafile offers built-in encryption that encrypts your files before they are uploaded to the server, thus keeping your data secure even if it's seized or stolen from the server. Even the system administrator of Seafile is unable to view the contents of your data.

Least Authority S4. S4 stands for "simple secure storage service" and is another example of a highly encrypted cloud service for individuals. Just as with Seafile, your data is encrypted before it leaves your computer; even the owner  of the server is unable to see its contents. As of this writing, Least Authority offers unlimited storage for only twenty-five dollars a month. The servers for Least Authority are hosted on Amazon's S3 platform in the United States, meaning that it is robust: even if a handful of the company's servers were dropped offline by fire, flood, other natural disasters, hackers, the NSA, or foreign governments, your data would still be safe and available to you. It includes features such as built-in versioning, which allows you to view previous revisions of your files, and seamless scalability due to the service's design on Amazon S3 servers, which support Microsoft Azure, Rackspace, Google, and Hewlett-Packard. Least Authority S4 also gives you full control over who can access your files and whether they can read from or write to individual files.

Now that we've talked about how to secure your files properly, both locally and on cloud storage, let's talk about how to properly and securely delete these files to make them inaccessible to anybody or any agency who's trying to recover them. When you delete a file from your computer, you are only deleting a small piece of information that tells the user where the file is stored on the hard drive. The file itself still exists on the physical media, but both the user and the operating system are blind to the file, making it appear that it was never there.

If you take a data-recovery tool (many of which are available on the internet), you can recover pretty much any file that has been "deleted." In the world of data recovery is where the difference between file deletion and file shredding comes into play. File shredding is just a term that we use to make users understand the concept of completely destroying the data that exists within a file. File shredding is really just writing over the file that exists on the physical media, thus rendering it irrecoverable. File-shredding applications overwrite this previously saved data with random data in a random order so that data-recovery software will be unable to recover the original content.

Debates on how many times you should overwrite a file have been going on forever. Some believe that you only need to overwrite the file once, while others insist that you must overwrite the file multiple times. The NSA insists that data be overwritten three times, while the US Department of Defense recommends seven. A 1990s paper written by a computer scientist named Peter Gutmann and his colleague Colin Plumb suggested that data should be overwritten thirty-five times to render it completely irrecoverable. The process of thirty-five rewrites is now known as the Gutmann method. I honestly believe that data should be safe when overwritten three to seven times. After all, the NSA designed the global surveillance system programs, so the agency should have the deepest understanding of how much data destruction is adequate.

Most file-shredding software can be run from right inside your operating system. These programs can scrub files from your recycle bin, erase your temporary internet files indefinitely, and even wipe the free space on your hard drive, which ensures that all your deleted files are completely scrubbed from the drive. My personal preference for full-disk file shredding is a program called Darik's Boot and Nuke, also known as DBAN. DBAN is a bootable tool that you can launch from either a USB or CD/ DVD and run on your computer's hard drive. DBAN allows you to choose whose standards to follow (i.e., the NSA's or the Gutmann method's) and how many passes to make when shredding your data.

To put into perspective how effective and essential file shredding is, I would like to refer to the example of "Topiary," who was the lead hacker in a group known as LulzSec. As part of his internet ban at his sentencing, he was also banned from using any file-shredding applications in the future. His having been banned from future file-shredding was so that if the FBI wanted to come in and audit his computer, they could. File shredding effectively removes your data for good.

Now that you've mastered encrypting data for storage and file delivery through text and email, it is important to know that your data can be stolen before you even save or encrypt your files. It is possible for hackers or government surveillance to install a keylogger, which monitors every key you type on the keyboard as you hit it. Keyloggers bypass all encryption methods because it takes place during the creation process. You can avoid this by (1) using the Tor live operating system since it completely erases itself and runs afresh at every boot; (2) not allowing installed keyloggers; and (3) checking your device regularly for hardware keyloggers.

CHAPTER 7

Password Management

• • •

TOO MANY PEOPLE USE THE same passwords over and over, which is the most insecure way to log into any web page, whether it's your social-media account or the bank that holds all your money. The reason many people do this is so they don't have to (or because they can't) remember separate passwords for all the sites they use. One of the best ways to combat this problem is by using a password manager. A password manager will store all the passwords to all the sites that you use on a daily basis. Some password managers even come with built-in password generators to generate the most secure passwords possible. Many of my passwords are forty characters or longer and are composed of random characters, numbers, and symbols. The password manager stores these passwords, which you can then access as needed. The password manager is then secured with one very secure password. If someone were to get ahold of your master password, then he or she would have access to all your sites. It is for this very reason that it is important to have a long and secure master password. My first recommendation to all my clients is to use a line of a favorite song, including spaces between words and capital letters for proper nouns. My second recommendation is not to use a line that includes the title of the song, such as "Welcome to the Hotel California."

Many password managers are available out there, including some that will auto-fill your websites and apps on your cellular device. Many are cross-platform, and many are ultra secure. The ones I will focus on in this chapter are both free and open-source. I cannot stress open-source software's security and safety enough. As I've explained numerous times, professionals and experts all over the world scrutinize previously open-source software because the code is open for anyone to examine; in contrast, closed software (that which is designed by companies) only gets examined by a few people and constantly has vulnerabilities for hackers and government entities to discover and exploit. Below I will discuss two separate password managers that I believe are best for you, the reader.

Master Password. This cross-platform program is based on a clever password-generating algorithm that ensures that your password will never be lost. Passwords are not stored inside this program, as with most password-managing programs; instead, they are generated on demand based on the name you use for this program. For this reason, master passwords are crossed to all devices without the need to sync, back up, or share passwords over the internet. Another great feature is that because passwords are generated algorithmically based on your full name and master password, you don't need to have internet access to retrieve any of your passwords. I suggest using Master Password and changing all the passwords you have used over and over again with new securely generated passwords you will never have to remember.

KeePass/KeePassX. This open-source and free password manager helps manage and store all your passwords in a highly secure way. All your passwords will be organized and stored in a single database instead of you writing them down in a book or on paper, constantly scratching them out and changing them. The database is locked and secured with a single master password. The database is then encrypted using the most secure algorithms currently known, which are AES and Twofish. KeePassX is the cross-platform version of KeePass. It does the same thing but works across devices and can store additional information such as URLs, attachments, and comments along with your usernames and passwords.

If you use the eight-character password that most sites require, a computer can go through all possible combinations and crack your password in less than a second, thus compromising the data behind your password. Using misspelled words with different letters or numbers is not enough to secure your valuable information. Snowden recommends that we all make a shift from passwords to passphrases. Passphrases are longer, which makes them more difficult to "brute force" (or crack through trying all possible combinations) and ensures that they cannot be compromised through a dictionary attack, which uses all the words in the dictionary and their combinations to crack passwords.

Now that you know how to secure and generate secure passwords, I challenge you to do it. Many people have been exposed to this information but decline to use it because it seems difficult.

What is it harder than—using the same password of "mypetdog-sname" for every website you belong to? Of course, it's harder than that, as it should be. It might seem hard, but if you start using this system today, it will seem second nature to you by next week.

CHAPTER 8

How to Obtain and Use Cryptocurrencies

• • •

LET ME START WITH WHAT cryptocurrency is. Cryptocurrency is a digital currency that is stored in a digital file known as a wallet. Cryptocurrencies do not go through banks and therefore are not subject to fees and other regulatory measures. Unlike paper money, cryptocurrency cannot just be printed at  will. There is a finite amount of each cryptocurrency, which is created through a process known as mining. Mining is a complex process that you do not need to understand to use Bitcoin, the most popular cryptocurrency, so we'll skip the complexities and save them for another book.

So how does one get cryptocurrency? Well, if you are technically savvy, you can use your computer's power to mine for it; or, if you are like most people, you can purchase it through a service by transferring money from your bank or credit card and purchasing it like you would a physical product. You can think of these companies as cryptocurrency banks. Here is a list of some of the most popular places to get cryptocurrency.

Coinbase. Easily the most popular here in the United States, Coinbase is an easy-to-use service that also works as an app on your smartphone. With Coinbase, you can purchase three different types of cryptocurrency, all of which have different values. You can purchase Bitcoin, Litecoin, or Ethereum. Just as with normal currency, these currencies go up and down in value. For example, Bitcoin has more than doubled in value in less than a year as of this writing.

LocalBitcoin. This service matches Bitcoin buyers with Bitcoin sellers. You meet up in person and exchange cash for Bitcoin. The service has been both wildly successful and unsuccessful at the same time; it has made it easier for anyone to buy Bitcoin, but it has also made it easy for criminals to rob people of their cash. One of the advantages of LocalBitcoin is that it is completely anonymous, and the Bitcoin you purchase is not linked to your name or bank account. We'll get into why this is important later.

BitQuick. This service claims to be the fastest way to purchase Bitcoin.

CoinCorner. This service requires users to verify their identity but then allows individuals to purchase cryptocurrency with both debit and credit cards.

BitBargain. This service offers many different payment methods and options for cryptocurrency buyers in the United Kingdom.

Xapo. This service claims to be the easiest way for users to buy Bitcoin and is known for its "cold-storage" vault.

These are a few of the options you can use to buy cryptocurrency. Many personally prefer to deal in Bitcoin, so from here on out, we'll discuss Bitcoin and how to use it to make anonymous transactions.

Once you've purchased Bitcoin, it becomes linked to your name and usually your bank account or credit card. One of the benefits of digital currency is that currency owners can use it in exchange for products and services anonymously, quickly, and without transaction fees. Other benefits are automatic, but you must first do a little work to make Bitcoin completely anonymous. Bitcoin (as well as all other cryptocurrencies) gets logged in a digital ledger every time it is transferred to and from someone, so to make it anonymous, you must use a technique known as tumbling. To do this, you must be on the Tor network either through the Tor browser inside Windows, Mac, or Linux or from the Tails live operating system briefly mentioned in the introduction to this book. The Tails live operating system is an operating system that resets itself each time it is restarted. Tails also incorporates many of the tools we've discussed in this book automatically; in this way, it keeps its users safe even if they have little to no technical knowledge.

Tumbling is the process of sending your Bitcoin into a central wallet along with other people's Bitcoins. These coins are then mixed or "tumbled." You are then sent different Bitcoins that are not attached to your name or banking information (minus a small tumbling fee).

If you were just to tumble the coins and send the new coins back to the same wallet that is identified as yours, then it wouldn't be anonymous. Instead, we'll go through a simple and secure process of completely anonymizing your Bitcoin.

1. Create an anonymous wallet. We'll call this wallet A. This should be done in a secure setting such as the Tails live operating system.
2. Send the Bitcoin you purchased (through whichever purchasing system you chose) to that wallet.
3. Create a second anonymous wallet. This will be the wallet you'll operate from; we'll call this wallet B.
4. From the first anonymous wallet, wallet A, you'll be sending your Bitcoin to a mixing or tumbling service. Many use a service called Helix Light, which is only accessible on the Tor network, but since you're using Tails, using that shouldn't be a problem.
5. You'll next have the Bitcoins sent back to wallet B. You'll see the option to delay when the coins are sent back so that they don't all arrive at once. You want to select that option. You also want to select the option to send them back to you in smaller increments; this ensures that your Bitcoins are more secure and anonymous.
6. Once you've completed these steps, your Bitcoins are now clean and ready for use.

I know you're probably wondering what you need anonymous Bitcoin for. Well, first things first, you should be using anonymous Bitcoin to purchase your VPN to maintain your anonymity. You may also want to make anonymous transactions or store money anonymously away from lurking eyes for a variety of reasons. Many places online will also take Bitcoin as payment. As of this writing, Japan has just made it a regular currency to use in local stores, and in the United States, you can now use Bitcoin on the web at Microsoft, Dell, Overstock, Newegg, TigerDirect, and other stores, with new stores getting on the bandwagon every day. Whatever your reasons for obtaining and storing anonymous currency may be, these reasons are your concern.

CHAPTER 9

PC Operating Systems and the Invincibility Mindset

• • •

I TELL PEOPLE OVER AND over again that they shouldn't use Windows or Mac if they're trying to be the most secure they can be. That eliminates the only two operating systems that most people know of. Why are these systems so insecure? Here's why. Because these systems are closed-source, they're not scrutinized as thoroughly, frequently, or extensively as open-source operating systems are. For this reason, they have a variety of exploitable vulnerabilities that can be used to steal your data and spy on your activities.

New reports have stated that the US government is the leading buyer of malware in the world. Instead of reporting these vulnerabilities to keep the public safe, the US government exploits them to capture its citizens' information and to spy on them. These vulnerabilities, known as zero-days (because the vulnerability has been protected against for zero days), cost the US government around $100,000 each. Any device with a microphone can be activated without indication, even if you have them turned off. Some "exploits" have been discovered that can listen to you through your phone's microphone to capture conversations, even when you've turned your device off. Other exploits turn on webcams in laptops without the user knowing. How many of you have an Amazon Echo, a TV you can talk to, or other smart-home devices with cameras and microphones?

The best way to avoid these vulnerabilities is to use an open-source alternative operating system. My personal preference is Qubes OS, which is capable of running Windows programs when needed.

 *Qubes OS.* This OS offers strong security and is open-source. Qubes is compartmentalized, which allows you to have separate virtual workspaces for work, school, home, banking, and whatever else you might want a separate virtual workstation for. One example where this type of compartmentalization is extremely useful is when you're opening email attachments. Say you receive an attachment from an untrusted source. You can open this email in a one-time-use compartmentalized "qube" and determine if the attachment is safe or not. Even if it contains a virus, nothing on your computer will be affected; once you're done using that "qube," everything is erased as if it never existed.

A quick web search will reveal a whole new world when it comes to OSs. Some of them are really good, and some of them are absolutely dreadful. If you'd like to use another OS and for some crazy reason you don't want to use Qubes, look for an open-source OS focused on privacy and security.

So far you've learned everything about file encryption: how to create encryption keys and avoid keyloggers, how to store encryption keys and prevent disclosure from hacks and seizures, and how to send encrypted data and emails without that information being vulnerable to exposure if that information is intercepted. Now I bet you feel invincible and that nothing can or will ever be tied to your digital presence or communication again. *Wrong.* Hackers and governments don't need to intercept communications to tie you to anything; they can simply wait for the mistakes that many of you will inevitably make, such as bragging on Facebook about illegal activity or being a member of a group that is under investigation. A simple subpoena at that point would do the trick. This has been the case many times before. One such example is when members of LulzSec were arrested after they were discovered to have sent files they had hacked and stolen, to one another, on Facebook in a message. No company is going to be bankrupted or go to jail for the sake of your privacy and security. You should consider everything you post or send online in clear text—meaning it is not encrypted—to now be in the hands of the NSA and hackers; they can now use that data to exploit you. This is where the nontechnical side of operational anonymization comes in.

Consider your online presence a completely different identity from your physical identity in the physical world. I do not advocate criminal actions, but for example, if you are buying something that could get you into trouble from an online dark-market site, provide yourself with adequate plausible deniability by acting as if your "pseudo identity" is making a purchase as a gift for your "real identity." If for some reason your pseudo identity is caught and tracked, this gives you room to imply that you have no control over what someone else does or sends to you. A message saying, "Let's send this to my friend's address, which is…" is a lot less incriminating than the same order with the message "My address is…"

Never use your real identity or the same identity across multiple sites. I believe it is impossible to make a username that doesn't tie back to your person or interests, so I recommend using a random password generator to generate usernames that are between five and eight characters long and are composed of random uppercase letters, lowercase letters, and numbers. This brings us back to the password-management program I spoke of earlier. These usernames are going to be hard to remember, and you better not be writing them down. Instead, store them in KeePassX, which is built into the Tails live operating system.

Are you the person who abbreviates everything, uses the same slang terms, uses four exclamation points after everything, and mistypes the same words all the time? It's time to change that behavior. If something is suspected of having been generated by you—whether it's a data leak, online order, or message—and it contains the same misspellings and bad grammar that all of your Facebook posts do, then these markers can be used to help correlate the activity to you. Always be sure to proofread and correct grammar on anything you do to prevent this from happening to you. It only takes one mistake.

What about the time when you use your computer? Do you always send your messages right when you wake up? Do you then leave the house, so that no activity is happening all day on that same account? Could someone who is watching you correlate these things? Many email programs now allow you to write messages and set the system to send them at another time. People who use their computers only during the day during specific hours give away their general location by time zone. Knowledge of your time zone alone is no big deal, but what other key information have you exposed that narrows down your location further and further?

CHAPTER 10

Metadata, EXIF Data, and Tracking Cookies

• • •

WORMER IS A PERFECT EXAMPLE of why it is important to understand metadata, which is hidden information about data (such as the date it was created and modified), and EXIF data (short for Exchangeable Image File), which is a specific type of metadata that a camera attaches to an image, such as the GPS coordinates and the model of camera used. W0rmer was a hacker/freedom fighter who would take pictures of his girlfriend and post them on pages he had defaced. Due to his lack of understanding of metadata and EXIF data, these actions led to his demise. The US government investigated the sites that had been defaced and examined the pictures that w0rmer had posted; the EXIF data within the pictures revealed the exact GPS location where each picture was taken. The metadata also exposed the type of camera lens that was used, and inside what kind of device the image was taken. The metadata brought the FBI knocking at w0rmer's girlfriend's door in Australia. If you're a freedom fighter, make sure you understand EXIF and metadata, so you don't join w0rmer in federal prison.

The Tails live operating system has tools that are intended to remove metadata, collectively called the Metadata Anonymization

Toolkit, or MAT. MAT supports a limited number of file types, which as of this writing include:

Portable Network Graphics (.png)
JPEG (.jpg, .jpeg, etc.)
Open Documents (.odt, .odx, .ods, etc.)
Office OpenXml (.docx, .pptx, .xlsx, etc.)
Portable Document Format (.pdf)
Tape ARchives (.tar, .tar.bz2, etc.)
MPEG Audio (.mp3, .mp2, .mp1, etc.)
Ogg Vorbis (.ogg)
Free Lossless Audio Codec (.flac)
Torrent (.torrent)

Nothing is perfect, and nothing should be relied on solely, so it is my recommendation not to post pictures of your girlfriend's cleavage on web pages that you have defaced.

Another case of a suspect being caught because of EXIF data is the case of John McAfee, who was arrested in Guatemala. McAfee agreed to do an interview with the magazine *Vice* titled "On the Run." The reporter took a picture with McAfee and included that photo in his article. The FBI then pulled the EXIF data from the picture, which was taken with a phone that had a GPS chip in it, which then led them to McAfee's front door.

In this case, I should restate my previous stance. It is a bad idea to post pictures after you've done something to cause others to chase you (to either injure or imprison you) without ensuring that you've erased the metadata and EXIF data. Even if someone is not actively searching for you, the information revealed in your hundreds of Facebook photos could give someone a good picture of your life to work with and make assumptions about. Stop handing over information freely that can be used against you.

Most of the time, we give away an incredible amount of information about ourselves without even realizing it; sometimes, the fact that we're giving our information away is obscured in a way that makes doing so seem good. Such is the case with tracking cookies. Tracking cookies sound very good. First, people love cookies, so something called a "cookie" sounds good to them. Second, cookies do things that we feel make life easier, such as storing passwords and allowing us to browse sites and then return to them later to resume where we left off. Stored passwords and resuming where you left off seems like a good thing, doesn't it? Have you ever realized that something you searched last week is now popping up all over your web browser in ads? What about the notes you saved in your personal notes file, which is shared between devices and transmitted via the internet? Yep, you guessed it: cookies.

Cookies are simply another way to track computer users and their identities. They store your passwords, your previous locations, and your search history; they allow web pages to determine which sites you have transferred to them from and which sites you are transferring to. By placing a tracking cookie on the computer of one individual, you can follow that person's entire browsing path, linking one site to the next and linking one account to another. If someone has two accounts on a media site—one for posting publicly and one for posting anonymously—and he or she accesses them from the same browser, then those accounts have just been linked, and that person will never be anonymous when using them. Your banking accounts and web history are all linked together and are used to make determinations about you as a person and your potential activities. Now that someone has linked your bank accounts, that person can see where you travel and every purchase you make and can place you in specific physical locations at any given point in time.

If for some reason you shop at the same grocery store, get fuel from the same station, and use the same bank as your local criminal, and your paths cross more than once by accident, then these activities have just unveiled a pattern of behavior that links both you and the criminal together. Now you're guilty by association. Sure, you could argue that you were simply in the wrong place at the wrong time, but by the time you're making this argument, you've already been targeted and are starting at a huge disadvantage in defending yourself against something you didn't even do.

CHAPTER 11

Always Keep a Backup

• • •

WHILE I WAS WRITING THIS book, I experienced the worst thing a secured computer could ever experience: my hard drive crashed. Because my hard drive was encrypted, I was unable to plug the hard drive into an external device to read it and extract data from it. Being unable to recover my data led me to write this chapter so that you can learn from my mistakes. Encrypting a hard drive makes it impossible for someone to pull the drive from your computer and to extract your data, which works both ways. The same applies to the drive you use to store your security and PGP keys. If you ever lose these, you can never restore them, and there is no "I forgot my password or key" option. If this happens, you'll be forced to abandon your data and start anew. Don't let this happen to you.

Make sure to keep a backup, and keep it in a safe location. It is often best practice to use the "three, two, one" backup method. "Three, two, one" means you should have three copies of your data, two different types of media, and one copy off-site. One example of this kind of setup would be to use both an external encrypted hard drive and an encrypted cloud-storage service. This configuration gives you the three copies I have suggested: one on your computer, one on your encrypted drive, and one in the cloud.

You have two different types of storage media—the encrypted external hard drive and the cloud—and one copy is off-site in the cloud, in case flood or fire destroys your computer and encrypted backup external drive.

Imagine having invested in Bitcoin. Bitcoin is constantly increasing in value: one Bitcoin purchased in January 2013 at $14 is worth $2,250 as of July 2017. So if you had invested $100 in Bitcoin in January 2013, your Bitcoin wallet would be worth approximately $16,071 today. Now imagine that your wallet was saved on your encrypted computer, and you had no backup. This wallet would be lost forever, with Bitcoin sitting in it, unable to ever be claimed again. Do you now understand the importance of maintaining good backups?

Since losing my data and my first edition of this very book, I have implemented a new backup plan, which I will share with you below. As you'll see, it uses the highly recommended three, two, one framework.

Seagate Expansion 1TB Portable External Hard Drive. This hard drive connects to your computer through USB 3.0, making it an extremely fast USB drive. I use NovaBackup to back up my computer daily, which includes an option to encrypt my backups.

Seafile. This service, which we went over in chapter 6, cost only ten dollars a month at the time of writing for up to 100 GB of data. Because I don't have more than 100 GB of data, I've chosen to go with this option. Should I require more space, I'll switch to Least Authority S4 for unlimited storage costing twenty-five dollars a month.

CHAPTER 12

Retaining an Attorney; Where Can You Run?

• • •

IF YOU FALL UNDER INVESTIGATION for whatever reason—whether you're a freedom fighter, a journalist breaking a very upsetting story (such as the mass-surveillance program), or a whistleblower—you may need the assistance of an attorney. In Snowden's case, to ensure the safety and security of his life and freedom, he felt it necessary to flee the United States. If you are planning an activity that could lead to this type of situation, it is important to plan ahead of time. Once the US government (or any government) has frozen your accounts and canceled your passport, it's too late.

After Snowden had released information about a secret US government program that spied on the activities and communications of all Americans in a manner that was in gross violation of civil liberties and rights, he fled the country. Before he landed in Russia, his passport was canceled, which trapped him in the airport of a foreign country and forced him to seek asylum. It wasn't long after that when his accounts were frozen, which caused his girlfriend (who was still living in his house at the time) to face eviction for nonpayment. Lucky for him, an attorney offered him pro bono services. Not everyone is this lucky.

So what should you do to prepare for this situation? First, it is important to consult and put an attorney on retainer. Speak with an attorney and be honest with him or her of your intentions. Agree on a fee that you will prepay to the attorney. This retainer provides you legal defense and a guarantee that your bond will be posted should you be detained.

If you do get detained, it is important to remain silent. If you've followed all the instructions in this book, then it is highly unlikely that the government agency will be capable of collecting enough information to detain you for very long. It doesn't matter what you are told in a detainment situation when you are being accused of something. Nothing you say can help you. If you are a US citizen, your Miranda rights clearly state that "anything you say can and will be used against you." In a court case, an officer cannot make any statements in your defense to help you. Once you admit guilt of any kind, you can guarantee further detainment and say good-bye to your freedom.

The police may switch tactics and begin to intimidate you by threatening large and cruel punishments and prison sentences. At least in the United States, police officers are permitted to lie to you in an interrogation to gain a confession. Don't fall for it. Simply remain silent. Again, if you follow all the advice in this book, the largest piece of evidence the police will be able to use against you will be your admission of guilt for a smaller sentence.

In some cases, you might feel it safer to run and flee from prosecution. Such was the case with Snowden, but where would you run? The following countries do not have extradition treaties with the United States, assuming that's where you're from. This is a good start but does not guarantee that you won't be shipped back to the United States:

Afghanistan, Algeria, Andorra, Angola, Armenia, Bahrain, Bangladesh, Belarus, Bosnia and Herzegovina, Brunei, Burkina Faso, Burma (Myanmar), Burundi, Cambodia, Cameroon, Cape Verde, the Central African Republic, Chad, China, Comoros, the Democratic Republic of the Congo (a.k.a. Congo-Kinshasa), Djibouti, Equatorial Guinea, Eritrea, Ethiopia, Gabon, Guinea, Guinea-Bissau, Indonesia, Ivory Coast, Kazakhstan, Kosovo, Kuwait, Laos, Lebanon, Libya, Macedonia, Madagascar, Maldives, Mali, Marshall Islands, Mauritania, Micronesia, Moldova, Mongolia, Montenegro, Morocco, Mozambique, Namibia, Nepal, Niger, Oman, Qatar, the Republic of the Congo (a.k.a. Congo-Brazzaville), Russia, Rwanda, Samoa, São Tomé and Príncipe, Saudi Arabia, Senegal, Serbia, Somalia, Sudan (a.k.a. North Sudan), Syria, Togo, Tunisia, Uganda, Ukraine, United Arab Emirates, Uzbekistan, Vanuatu, the Vatican, Vietnam, and Yemen.

Again, the lack of an extradition agreement does not guarantee that you will not be extradited, but you would be much safer choosing a country that does not have a pre-made agreement to send you back upon request. One such example is Cambodia. Despite the fact that Cambodia does not have an extradition treaty, its government extradited a known pirate and copyright violator named Gottfrid Svartholm back to Sweden.

Another example of a known pirate fleeing from prosecution is in the case of Fredrik Neij, who fled to Laos. In this case, Neij was convicted of helping to make copyright content available. Unlike the case of Svartholm, Neij was not extradited and was allowed to remain in Laos.

CHAPTER 13

Learning from
Others' Mistakes

• • •

IN A PREVIOUS CHAPTER, YOU may remember me referring to a group of hacktivists by the name LulzSec. The leader of this group went by the name of Sabu. This group has taken credit for security exploitation of many online servers and then posting their information on a public site called PasteBin, which is used to share information. This group has officially been charged with hacking the Fox Broadcasting Company, Sony Entertainment, and PBS.

For communication, the group started an IRC (or internet relay chat) in which members discussed their attacks and exploits. Sabu often bragged through Facebook of his success in selling stolen credit cards. Besides hacking these major companies and defacing their websites, members of LulzSec also hacked and leaked the identities of many law-enforcement officers, hacked Sony users, and caused mayhem online, including mounting a DDOS (or distributed denial of service attack), an attack in which hackers use computers to send tons of information to a server in order to overload it, against the Central Intelligence Agency.

At the time, Sabu was one of the best and most well-known hackers and was wanted by every major intelligence agency in the United States. The FBI would eventually catch him and threaten him with 112 years in prison. So how was he caught? Sabu made just one mistake and one day logged into an IRC from his real IP address. Had he been using Tor, he would not have been caught. He turned informant on the same day he was captured. Sabu was an unemployed computer programmer who was collecting welfare and had two young children to care for, which is how the FBI got him to flip so quickly. Once Sabu was working for the FBI, it took no time at all to capture all of his friends as well.

On the day after Christmas, Sabu discussed in the IRC the "Stratfor" hack and the thirty thousand credit card numbers they had stolen. Stratfor is a high-profile private-investigation company that many well-known companies and the US government have hired in the past. Many retired intelligence officers work for Stratfor, and the hackers used the retired FBI agents' credit cards to make major donations to different charities. While Sabu discussed these activities with his colleagues, he was using a government-issued laptop that recorded everything.

Sabu began to engage one of his colleagues by the name of "sup_g." Sabu knew of many other names that sup_g went by and needed to connect the identities for the FBI. To do this, Sabu referred to sup_g by another of his identities, "anarchaos," by saying that "if I get raided anarchaos your job is to cause havoc in my honor." Sup_g replied with "it shall be so." You should be using multiple identities in your online world, and you should be extremely careful never to let those identities cross over. Be very wary if anyone ever refers to you by an identity other than the one you are currently active on.

Besides this attempt to link multiple user identities, Sabu also forfeited his logs to the FBI, where the agency found some identifying information that Sabu's friends had shared with him. On August 29, 2011, Sabu's friend sup_g, who also went by "burn" in addition to "anarchaos," had stated that his friends had been arrested in Saint Louis a few weeks earlier "for midwestrising tar sands work." His message gave the FBI a general location (the Midwest) of where he might live. Another of sup_g's accounts had mentioned to Sabu that he had once been arrested in New York City for protesting in 2004. Another of sup_g's accounts, "yohoho," had stated that he hadn't been back to New York since his arrest at the Republican National Convention in 2004. Armed with this information, the FBI searched New York City police lists of arrestees from that conference; the agency found that a Midwesterner named Jeremy Hammond had been detained at the convention. Sup_g and "burn" had both indicated to Sabu that they had spent time in prison, and burn specified that it had been a federal penitentiary. A background check on Jeremy Hammond revealed this same fact. Sup_g never knew when to stop talking; he later revealed to Sabu that he had spent a few weeks in jail for being caught with marijuana but asked Sabu not to tell anyone, because "it could compromise my identity." If you have to tell someone not to share information because it would compromise your identity, then why would you say anything? Keep your mouth shut.

Now that the FBI had a general suspicion about Jeremy Hammond, they monitored his Wi-Fi and found his MAC (or media access control) address. Previously, Jeremy had revealed to Sabu that he used an Apple computer, and the MAC address the FBI found belonged to an Apple computer. (Note that a MAC can belong to any computer, not just Macs.) Now that the FBI was sitting on the Hammond house, agents called Sabu every time

Hammond left to verify that the suspected account had indeed gone offline. The government then used this evidence in a trial to help convict Jeremy Hammond of violating the "Computer Fraud and Abuse Act" and to put him in jail for ten years.

CHAPTER 14

Evidence That Operational Anonymization Works

• • •

I MUST ADMIT THAT OPERATIONAL anonymization, like anything else in this world, can be used for bad as well as good. Drugs are used to treat illnesses, but some people abuse them; police keep the public safe, but some are corrupt; privacy and security keep people safe but also keep criminals safe from prosecution.

Due to my extreme disgust of the particular type of crime discussed below, I will omit the actual crime from this chapter. Instead, I'll go through how the leaders of this group managed to evade detection and arrest. They remain free to this day. The actors in this crime are among the most highly wanted people in the world, pursued by every police agency and intelligence agency on earth. Various federal agencies hunt them continuously and punish them severely when they catch them, as they should. This chapter is not meant to teach you to commit crimes and not get caught; it is simply a demonstration of how even the most wanted criminals in the world can use these exact tactics and tools to remain free.

This criminal group was operational for more than six years, during which the group shared 411,000 files between them and stored the files on a central server the group operated. The reason we know this exact information is that the FBI worked strenuously for fifteen months to infiltrate the criminal group in the hope of detecting and arresting its members. Not every member of the criminal group was versed in the tools we've discussed in this book, so the FBI was able to arrest 30 percent of its members. The leader of the group, however, has remained free.

The FBI's report stated that it faced a number of challenges during "Operation Achilles":

The group utilized an unprecedented level of organization and sophistication. They had a timed test for prospective new members. They had to use encryption technology and internet-based anonymizers, remailing [a service that anonymously forwards emails to keep users anonymous] services. They also intentionally corrupted their files, and only the new members knew how to reconfigure those files to be able to read the [files]. They also had the uncanny ability to monitor worldwide news pertaining to law enforcement efforts...and matters in order to better educate themselves to avoid law enforcement detection.

So how do we know the leader of the group is still free and has not been detained for his crimes? The leader made several appearances on Usenet, which is a noncentralized computer network (like a public Facebook) that discusses topics such as newsgroups and securely sharing files. He did so on the anniversary of the FBI bust that captured some of the members, and he answered people's questions. One of the things he mentioned in his discussions was that everyone who used Tor and remailers remained free. He also pointed out that his co-leaders had not used Tor and had relied solely on a VPN to keep them anonymous. Both of them are now in prison, one serving twenty-five years in the United Kingdom and one serving life in an Arizona prison.

VPN services are for privacy, not for anonymity. They keep your data safe, but they do not secure your identity. To stay hidden, you need both privacy and anonymity, and that is what operational anonymization is exactly. As I've said before, no business or individual will go to jail for a customer who pays twenty dollars a month.

The second way users were getting caught was that they had become too complacent in their security within the group. They became so comfortable that they began to lessen their guard by disclosing information that could tie their real identities to their digital identities. Even though these messages were encrypted, they were sending them to people whom the police had arrested and seized the private keys of, thus allowing them to decrypt the messages. This is another example of why it is important to keep your real identity and digital identity separate and not share any personal information through your digital identity. No matter how much you trust your criminal friends, you always face the risk that the police will catch them and seize their computers; if they're given the option of a lesser sentence in exchange for handing over their encryption keys, they will do just that, much like Sabu did to Jeremy Hammond.

This group had a very strict set of rules (paraphrased below), which included the following:

* Never reveal your true identity to another member of the group.
* Never communicate with another member of the group outside the Usenet channel.
* Group membership must remain strictly within the confines of the internet.

- No member is able to identify another positively.
- Members do not reveal personally identifying information.
- The primary communications newsgroup must regularly be migrated. (A newsgroup is "a discussion about a particular subject consisting of notes written to a central internet site and distributed through Usenet.")

The FBI never caught members who abided by these strict rules. The FBI had completely penetrated the group, but due to the security protocols the group had in place, the FBI was still unable to identify and prosecute many of the members of the group.

I must again state that this is not a book intended for criminals to begin an enterprise and avoid detection by local and federal authorities. I have included this simply to show how effective these tools are even against agencies that are working cooperatively across jurisdictions and countries and that have unlimited workforce and funds. At such high levels of perseverance, due to the nature of the crime, even the executive assistant FBI director, J. Stephen Tidwell, was involved in the investigation. These tools thwarted a combined effort by the FBI, Europol, and Interpol. You cannot design a method to keep some people safe while allowing that method to expose others (such as criminals). Either everyone is safe, or no one is safe.

Bibliography

• • •

DeepDotWeb. "PGP Tutorial for Windows (Kleopatra-Gpg-4Win)." November 3, 2015. Accessed July 8, 2017. https://www.deepdotweb.com/2015/02/21/pgp-tutorial-for-windows-kleopatra-gpg4win/.

DeepDotWeb. "Security Tutorials." Deep Dot Web. Accessed July 8, 2017. https://www.deepdotweb.com/security-tutorials/.

Mozilla. "Build Technology Idea Submission [Hide IP]." Issue #2. Mozilla/TBTWBuildChallenge. GitHub. Accessed July 8, 2017. https://github.com/mozilla/TBTWBuildChallenge/issues/2.

"Privacy Tools | Encryption against Global Mass Surveillance." Privacytools.io. Accessed July 08, 2017. https://privacytoolsio.github.io/privacytools.io/.

Project, Inc. "Tor." Tor Browser. Accessed July 8, 2017. https://www.torproject.org/projects/torbrowser.html.

Rodger, Jolly. "Jolly Roger's Security Thread for Beginners." The Hub. January 15, 2014. Accessed July 08, 2017. http://thehub-b7xbw4dc5r2.onion/index.php?topic=52.0.

Tails Installation Assistant. "Download and Verify the Tails ISO Image." Accessed July 8, 2017. https://tails.boum.org/install/win/usb/index.en.html.

Appendixes

• • •

How to Set Up Tails

• • •

YOU WILL NEED TWO USB sticks (4 GB or larger) and about two hours. The following instructions, which I have paraphrased here, are available online.[2]

DOWNLOAD AND VERIFY THE TAILS ISO IMAGE

In this step, you will download Tails as an ISO image: a single file containing the whole operating system. For your security, it is very important to verify your download. I propose two techniques to do this verification automatically. You can download the ISO image via the Firefox add-on. The add-on verifies your download automatically.

INSTALL AN INTERMEDIARY TAILS

In this step, you will install an intermediary Tails by copying the Tails ISO image on the first USB stick using a program called Universal USB Installer.

* Plug the first USB stick into the computer.

---

2 Tails Installation Assistant. "Download and Verify the Tails ISO Image." Accessed July 8, 2017. https://tails.boum.org/install/win/usb/index.en.html.

* Click on the following link to download Universal USB Installer: https://git-tails.immerda.ch/uui-binary/plain/Universal-USB-Installer.exe.
* At the Windows security warning, confirm that you want to run the program.
* Read the license agreement and click "I Agree" to continue and start Universal USB Installer.
* Select Tails from the drop-down list.
* Click Browse and choose the ISO image that you down-loaded earlier.
* Use the drop-down list to specify the USB stick on which you want to install the ISO image.
* Select the "Fat32 Format Drive" option.
* Click Create.
* A warning appears. Click Yes to start the installation. The installation takes a few minutes.
* After the installation is finished, click Close to quit Universal USB Installer.

You now have an intermediary Tails on your first USB stick. You will soon have to restart your computer on this USB stick. It can be a bit tricky, so good luck.

RESTART ON THE INTERMEDIARY TAILS

* Shut down the computer while leaving the first USB stick plugged in.
* Switch on the computer.
* If the computer starts on Tails, the Boot Loader menu appears. Choose Tails and press Enter.

- Click on the following link to download Universal USB Installer: https://git-tails.immerda.ch/uui-binary/plain/Universal-USB-Installer.exe.
- At the Windows security warning, confirm that you want to run the program.
- Read the license agreement and click "I Agree" to continue and start Universal USB Installer.
- Select Tails from the drop-down list.
- Click Browse and choose the ISO image that you downloaded earlier.
- Use the drop-down list to specify the USB stick on which you want to install the ISO image.
- Select the "Fat32 Format Drive" option.
- Click Create.
- A warning appears. Click Yes to start the installation. The installation takes a few minutes.
- After the installation is finished, click Close to quit Universal USB Installer.

You now have an intermediary Tails on your first USB stick. You will soon have to restart your computer on this USB stick. It can be a bit tricky, so good luck.

RESTART ON THE INTERMEDIARY TAILS

- Shut down the computer while leaving the first USB stick plugged in.
- Switch on the computer.
- If the computer starts on Tails, the Boot Loader menu appears. Choose Tails and press Enter.

How to Set Up Tails

• • •

YOU WILL NEED TWO USB sticks (4 GB or larger) and about two hours. The following instructions, which I have paraphrased here, are available online.[2]

DOWNLOAD AND VERIFY THE TAILS ISO IMAGE

In this step, you will download Tails as an ISO image: a single file containing the whole operating system. For your security, it is very important to verify your download. I propose two techniques to do this verification automatically. You can download the ISO image via the Firefox add-on. The add-on verifies your download automatically.

INSTALL AN INTERMEDIARY TAILS

In this step, you will install an intermediary Tails by copying the Tails ISO image on the first USB stick using a program called Universal USB Installer.

* Plug the first USB stick into the computer.

---

2   Tails Installation Assistant. "Download and Verify the Tails ISO Image." Accessed July 8, 2017. https://tails.boum.org/install/win/usb/index.en.html.

7. You can choose which Start Menu folder you want it installed in; just click Next.
8. It will now install. Click Next, then Finish.

Now you have the tools you need to get started with PGP. The next step is to generate your key pair so that you can encrypt and decrypt messages. We'll go with 4096-bit RSA.

1. Open up Kleopatra.
2. Go to File, then New Certificate
3. The Certificate Creation Wizard should pop up. Click on "Create a personal OpenPGP key pair."
4. Now you'll enter your details. Use your marketplace username as "Name" and fill out the rest with whatever you want. You don't need to use a real email address. **Do not click Next yet.** We need to fill out a few more details first. Click "Advanced Settings…" Another window should appear. Under Key Material, make sure RSA is checked. In the drop-down menu beside it, select 4,096 bits. Check the picture to confirm that you have everything set correctly, then click OK.
5. Confirm that you've filled out all your information correctly, then click Create Key.
6. Another window will pop up asking you to enter a passphrase. Do so, then click OK.
7. It will now generate your key. It will need you to do random things to create entropy: mash the keys on your keyboard, wiggle the mouse—you name it.
8. Your key is now created. Go ahead and click Finish.

How to Generate PGP Keys

• • •

THE FOLLOWING HAS BEEN MODIFIED somewhat from an online link.[3] GPG4Win is one of the best and easiest ways to generate secure PGP inside of Windows.

1. Go to https://gpg4win.org/download.html. We want the full version, so click Gpg4win 2.2.3.
2. Save it; open it when it's done downloading. If you have UAC (User Account Controls) enabled, click Yes on the window that appears.
3. Choose your language; click OK.
4. Click Next and then Next again. You'll now see a screen asking what components you want to install. Select Kleopatra, GpgEX, GPA, and Gpg4win Compendium. Then click Next.
5. It will ask where to install them; just keep the default and click Next.
6. Now it'll ask where you want to install the shortcuts. Select whichever you want and click Next.

---

3 DeepDotWeb. "PGP Tutorial for Windows (Kleopatra-Gpg4Win)." November 3, 2015. Accessed July 8, 2017. https://www.deepdotweb.com/2015/02/21/pgp-tutorial-for-windows-kleopatra-gpg4win/.

* Click on the Create button.
* Wait for the creation to finish.
* The assistant shows a list of possible persistence features. Each feature corresponds to a set of files or settings to be saved in the encrypted persistent storage.
* Click Save.

RESTART AND ACTIVATE THE PERSISTENT STORAGE

* Shut down the computer and restart on the second Tails USB stick.
* In Tails Greeter:
  * Select your preferred language in the drop-down list on the bottom left of the screen.
  * In the "Use persistence?" section, choose Yes to activate the encrypted persistent storage for the current working session.
  * Enter the passphrase of the persistent volume in the Passphrase text box.
  * Click Login.
* After fifteen to thirty seconds, the Tails desktop appears.
* You can now save personal files and working documents in the Persistent folder. To open the Persistent folder, choose Places ▶ Persistent.

- In the Boot Loader menu, choose Tails and press Enter.
- After thirty to sixty seconds, Tails Greeter appears.
- In Tails Greeter, select your preferred language in the drop-down list on the bottom left of the screen. Click Login.
- After fifteen to thirty seconds, the Tails desktop appears.

You're done installing Tails!

CREATE AN ENCRYPTED PERSISTENT STORAGE (OPTIONAL)

You have the option to create encrypted persistent storage in the remaining free space on the second Tails USB stick to store any of the following:

- personal files and working documents
- some of your settings
- your encryption keys

The data in the encrypted persistent storage remains available across separate working sessions and is encrypted using a passphrase of your choice.

CREATE THE PERSISTENT STORAGE

- Choose Applications ▸ Tails ▸ Configure persistent volume.
- Specify a passphrase of your choice in both the Passphrase and Verify Passphrase text boxes.

* After thirty to sixty seconds, another screen called Tails Greeter appears.
* In Tails Greeter, select your preferred language in the drop-down list on the bottom left of the screen. Click Login.
* After fifteen to thirty seconds, the Tails desktop appears.

The most difficult part is over. Now grab your second USB stick, as it is time to install the final Tails on it.

INSTALL THE FINAL TAILS

In this step, you'll install the final Tails on a second USB stick using Tails Installer.

* Plug the second USB stick into the computer.
* Choose Applications ▸ Tails ▸ Tails Installer to start Tails Installer.
* Click on the Install by Cloning button.
* Choose the second USB stick in the Target Device drop-down list.
* To start the installation, click on the Install Tails button.
* Read the warning message in the confirmation dialog. Click Yes to confirm.
* Close Tails Installer.

RESTART ON THE FINAL TAILS

* Shut down the computer.
* Unplug the first USB stick and leave the second USB stick plugged in.
* Switch on the computer.

Now we need to get your public key. Without it, people will not be able to send you secure messages.

1. Right-click on your key; then click "Export Certificates..."
2. Browse where you want to save, give it a name, and then click Save.
3. Open your favorite text editor and browse to where the file is saved. You may have to select "All files" from the dropdown menu. Click the file you saved, then open it.
4. There's your public key. Remember to add your public key to your market profile so people can message you more easily.

The next step, obtaining your private key, is as easy as obtaining your public key. Right-click on your public key and select "Export Secret Keys..."

1. Select where you want the private key saved, give it a name, check ASCII armor, and click OK.
2. You now have your private key.

Remember to keep this in a safe place, and never share it!

It's impossible to send a vendor an encrypted message without the vendor's public key.

1. Find a public key you want to import.
2. Copy everything from "BEGIN PGP PUBLIC KEY BLOCK" to "END PGP PUBLIC KEY BLOCK."
3. In your task bar, right-click on the Kleopatra icon, go to Clipboard and then click Certificate Import.

4. If it worked, you should see a window pop up; click OK.
5. You should now see the imported key in Kleopatra under the Other Certificates tab.

Now you have to import your private key.

1. Go to File; then click "Import Certificates…"
2. Browse to where your private key is, select it, and then click Open.
3. The program will import your private key and pop up a window to confirm. Click OK.
4. You should now see your key information under the My Certificates tab.

Now that you're ready to go, it's time to send a message.

1. Open up your text editor of choice.
2. Type out your message, select it all, and copy it.
3. In your task bar, right-click on the Kleopatra icon, go to Clipboard, and then click "Encrypt…"
4. A beautiful window will open. Click "Add Recipient…"
5. Another window will appear. Click the Other Certificates tab, then select who you want to send your message to and click OK.
6. You should be back to the previous window with the recipient listed. Click Next.
7. Click OK.
8. Your encrypted message will be in your clipboard; all you need to do is paste it into the message box and send.

Decrypting messages is just as easy as encrypting.

1. Copy everything that you sent.
2. In your task bar, right-click on the Kleopatra icon, go to Clipboard, and then click "Decrypt/Verify..."
3. A window will pop up asking for your passphrase; enter that and then click OK.
4. A window should pop up verifying that your message was decrypted and copied to your clipboard. Click Finish.
5. Open your text editor of choice and paste in your message.

How to Install and Use Tor

• • •

THE FOLLOWING INSTRUCTIONS ARE ALSO paraphrased from an on-line source.[4] Using the program Tor Browser allows you to use Tor on Windows, Mac OSX, or Linux without needing to install any software. It can run off a USB flash drive, it comes with a pre-configured web browser to protect your anonymity, and it's self-contained (i.e., it can be placed on a USB flash drive and run on any computer). Download the Tor Brower from https://www.torproject.org.

* Click Run, then choose the installer's language and click OK.
* Make sure you have at least 80 MB of free disk space in the location you select. If you want to leave the bundle on the computer, saving it to the desktop is a good choice. If you want to move it to a different computer or limit the traces you leave behind, save it to a USB drive instead.
* Click Install. Wait until the installer finishes, which may take a few minutes to complete.

---

4 Project, Inc. "Tor." Tor Browser. Accessed July 8, 2017. https://www.torproject.org/projects/torbrowser.html.

- Once the installation is complete, click Finish to launch the Tor Browser wizard.
- Once you see the Tor Browser wizard, click Connect.
- Alternatively, you can launch Tor Browser by going to the folder Tor Browser, which can be found at the location where you saved the bundle (default: desktop); double-click on the "Start Tor Browser" application.
- Once Tor is ready, Tor Browser will automatically be opened. Only web pages you visit through Tor Browser will be sent via Tor. Other web browsers (such as internet Explorer) are not affected.
- Once you're finished browsing, close any open Tor Browser windows by clicking on the red X. For privacy reasons, the list of web pages you visited and any cookies will be deleted.
- To use Tor Browser again, double-click on the "Start Tor Browser" application.

Remember that Tor anonymizes the origin of your traffic and encrypts everything inside the Tor network, but it can't encrypt your traffic between the Tor network and the traffic's final destination. If you're communicating sensitive information, you should use as much care as you would on the normal internet: use HTTPS or other end-to-end encryption and authentication.

How to Choose
the Right VPN

• • •

VPNs HAVE MAJOR ADVANTAGES WHEN used correctly. In addition to providing privacy, VPNs are good for:

* hiding your internet usage from your internet service provider as well as law-enforcement and government agencies;
* downloading torrents such as music, movies, and software without detection;
* bypassing country blocks on media streaming services (some VPNs allow this);
* protecting your information from hackers when using Wi-Fi;
* using on any device.

All this being said, VPNs are only as secure as the companies running them and the users putting data into them. Not all VPNs are equally secure. Some VPNs log all your activity, which defeats the purpose of using a VPN.

I have compiled a list of VPNs that I believe are safe for protecting your privacy and anonymity alongside Tor. Keep in mind that VPN companies have claimed not to keep logs before but have still handed information over to the US government, so use caution with everything you say or send over the internet, even when using a VPN. Always encrypt your data. I recommend:

1. IPVanish
2. NordVPN
3. StrongVPN
4. OverPlay
5. PrivateVPN

All the VPNs listed here claim not to keep any logs, and most accept Bitcoin as an anonymous form of payment, which ups your security to the next level. If you purchase something through Bitcoin, the cryptocurrency protects you even if the VPNs do keep logs by not allowing the VPNs to tie the account back to a specific person. None of these companies have ever assisted or turned over information in any legal proceeding.

APPENDIX E

How to Securely
Wipe a Drive

• • •

As I MENTIONED EARLIER, MY personal preference for full-disk file shredding is a program called Darik's Boot and Nuke, also known as DBAN. DBAN needs to be booted on the computer with the drive you want to wipe, so first we'll have to set up the bootable tool you'll be using. You can do this on the same computer (if it still runs).

* Download DBAN to your computer.
* Burn DBAN to a disc or create a bootable USB.
* Boot the computer with the drive you wish to wipe from your bootable disc or USB with DBAN.
* Choose your desired option from the main menu. For the quick method of erasing every hard drive that's plugged in, you'll want to press the F3 key; hitting Enter will bring you to a menu where you'll have a little more control.
* If you choose to wipe all drives and press F3, follow with the "Autonuke" command to begin wiping.

* If you chose to press Enter, you will be asked which drives you would like to wipe. Use K and J to go up and down the list, and press Space to select the drive.
* Once you've selected your drive, you see the advanced options. Press M to choose which method you'd like to use in wiping your drive. Choose "DoD Short."

Once the process has completed, you'll see a "DBAN succeeded" message. At this point, you're finished, and the drive is completely erased.